INTRODUCTORY
LOGIC

ANSWER KEY

Third Edition
Revised and Expanded

Douglas J. Wilson
James B. Nance

Canon Press

MOSCOW, IDAHO

The Mars Hill Textbook Series

Introductory Logic, Douglas J. Wilson & James B. Nance
Intermediate Logic, James B. Nance
Latin Primer: Book I, Martha Wilson
Latin Primer: Book II, Martha Wilson
Latin Primer: Book III, Martha Wilson
Latin Grammar: Book I, Douglas J. Wilson & Karen Craig

———————————————

Douglas J. Wilson & James B. Nance, *Introductory Logic for Christian Private and Home Schools—Answer Key*

© 1997 by Douglas Wilson & James B. Nance.
Published by Canon Press, P.O. Box 8741, Moscow, ID 83843
800-488-2034

First Edition, 1990; Second Edition 1992; Third Edition 1997

Printed in the United States of America.

ISBN: 1-885767-36-6

Table of Contents
Logic Key

STATEMENTS AND
THEIR RELATIONSHIPS

Exercise One

Examine the following sentences and determine whether or not they are statements. In the space provided, write down true statement, false statement, question, command, or nonsense. Be careful.

1. Jesus healed blind men.   `True Statement`

2. King David was the first king of Israel.   `False Statement`

3. The tongues of flame at Pentecost were water.   `False Statement`

4. Who wrote the book of Hebrews?   `Question`

5. Children, obey your parents.   `Command`

6. The Bible is the Word of God.   `True Statement`

7. The Great Pyramid is six feet high.   `False Statement`

8. Who said slaves should obey their masters?   `Question`

9. How old was Jesus when He was baptized?   `Question`

10. The slithy toves did gyre and gimble.   `Nonsense`

11. Believe the good news.   `Command`

12. The United States has fifty states.   `True Statements`

Brain teaser: God does not exist.

`Some would consider this strictly nonsense, because if it were true that God did not exist, then rational statements could not exist. But "God does not exist" purports to be a rational statement. So if it were right, there would be no reason to believe it—because God is the foundation of reason. However, if we consider it false, then we are claiming that God *does* exist and thus so do false statements. So this statement cannot be true. It is either false or nonsense.`

Exercise Two

1. List below five examples of a phrase which would introduce a self-report, such as, "In my opinion..."

```
I think . . .
I believe . . .
I feel . . .
I thought . . .
I want . . .
```

2. List below five statements of your own which are true or false by logical structure. Include at least one tautology and one self-contradiction.

```
The sun is shining, or it is not.
I will go to school, or I will not.
The book is red, and it is not red.
The flipped coin will come up heads and hot heads.
A man can either tell a joke, or he can't.
```

3. List below five statements which are true or false by definition.

```
Bachelors are unmarried men.
Bachelors are little girls.
This square is a four-sided figure.
This square is a five-sided figure.
My uncle is my relative.
```

Exercise Three

Examine each of the following statements. In the blank at the right, enter the type of statement you believe it to be. Your options are *self-report,* self-supporting by *logical structure,* self-supporting by *definition,* and *supported.*

1. *The snow is deep.*   Supported

2. *I think Jesus is not what He claimed.*   Self-report

3. *Paul was an apostle, or he wasn't.*   Logical Structure

4. *Jericho fell to the invading Israelites.*   Supported

5. *I believe David really loved Bathsheba.*   Self-report

6. *A square has four sides.*   Definition

7. *Genesis is the first book of the Bible.*   Supported

8. *Jesus is God, and He is not God.*   Logical Structure

9. *Jesus is God, and He is man.*   Supported

10. *I think the snow is deeper than last year.*   Self-report

11. *Jeremiah was a reluctant prophet.*   Supported

12. *My mother is a woman.*   Definition

13. *It either works, or it doesn't.*   Logical Structure

14. *Herod was an evil tyrant.*   Supported

15. *The New Testament was written in Greek.*   Supported

Exercise Four

With the following five sets of statements, circle Y if the statements are consistent, circle N if they are not consistent.

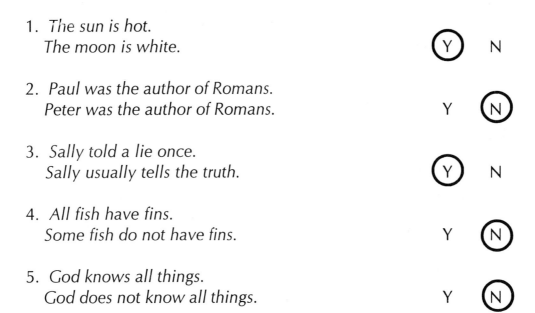

1. *The sun is hot.*
   The moon is white.   (Y)   N

2. *Paul was the author of Romans.*
   Peter was the author of Romans.   Y   (N)

3. *Sally told a lie once.*
   Sally usually tells the truth.   (Y)   N

4. *All fish have fins.*
   Some fish do not have fins.   Y   (N)

5. *God knows all things.*
   God does not know all things.   Y   (N)

With the next five sets of statements, circle Y if the first sentence implies the second, circle N if it does not.

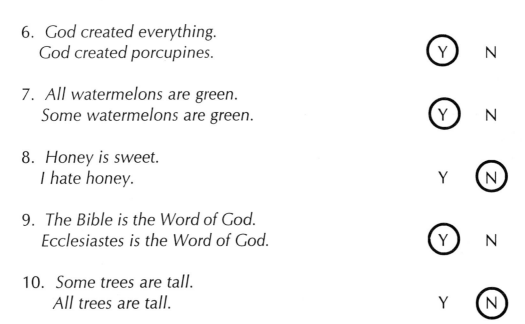

6. *God created everything.*
   God created porcupines.   (Y)   N

7. *All watermelons are green.*
   Some watermelons are green.   (Y)   N

8. *Honey is sweet.*
   I hate honey.   Y   (N)

9. *The Bible is the Word of God.*
   Ecclesiastes is the Word of God. (Y)   N

10. *Some trees are tall.*
    All trees are tall.   Y   (N)

Now seek to determine whether the statements in these sets are logically equivalent. If they are equivalent, circle Y, if not circle N.

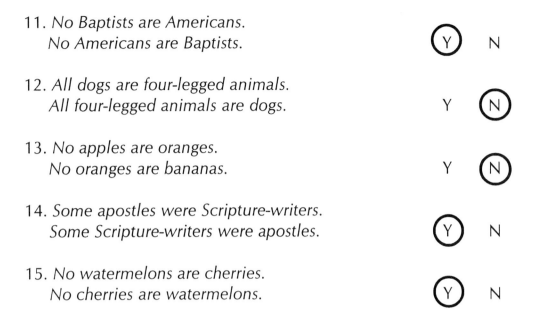

11. *No Baptists are Americans.*
    No Americans are Baptists.   (Y)   N

12. *All dogs are four-legged animals.*
    All four-legged animals are dogs.   Y   (N)

13. *No apples are oranges.*
    No oranges are bananas.   Y   (N)

14. *Some apostles were Scripture-writers.*
    Some Scripture-writers were apostles.   (Y)   N

15. *No watermelons are cherries.*
    No cherries are watermelons.   (Y)   N

Lastly, examine these sets to determine independency. Circle Y if the statements are independent, circle N if they are not independent.

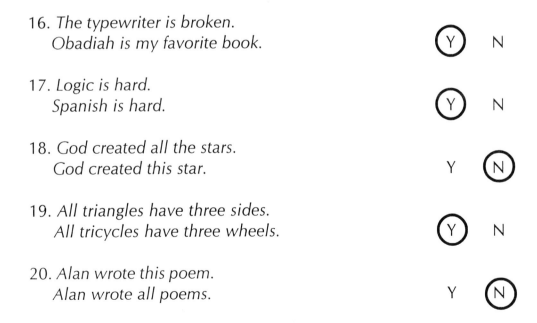

16. *The typewriter is broken.*
    Obadiah is my favorite book.   (Y)   N

17. *Logic is hard.*
    Spanish is hard.   (Y)   N

18. *God created all the stars.*
    God created this star.   Y   (N)

19. *All triangles have three sides.*
    All tricycles have three wheels.   (Y)   N

20. *Alan wrote this poem.*
    Alan wrote all poems.   Y   (N)

Exercise Five

Give examples of the three types of disagreements.

Real disagreement

1. Luther: **No man has free will.**

   Erasmus: **Some men have free will.**

2. Lee: **The South had the right to secede.**

   Grant: **The South did not have the right to secede.**

Apparent disagreement

3. Peter: **I think I should go to Rome.**

   Paul: **I think you should stay in Jerusalem.**

4. Homer: **I believe Zeus is king of the gods.**

   Virgil: **I believe Jupiter is king of the gods.**

Verbal disagreement

5. William: **All of Scotland must go to war.**

   Robert: **No, only the men of Scotland should go to war.**

6. Write two statements which are consistent but not independent.

   All Christians are forgiven sinners.

   Some Christians are forgiven sinners.

Exercise Six

In the blank below each sentence, rewrite the sentence using only the verb of being.

1. *John eats turnips.*
   John is a turnip eater.

2. *Rebekah reads her Bible daily.*
   Rebekah is a daily Bible reader.

3. *Paul resisted Peter and Barnabas.*
   Paul was a Peter and Barnabus resister.

4. *Susan works hard to resist temptation.*
   Susan is a hard-working temptation resister.

5. *Faith produces fruit.*
   Faith is a fruit producer.

6. *The works of the sinful nature lead to death.*
   The works of the sinful nature are to-death leaders.

7. *The donkey rebuked the prophet.*
   The donkey was a prophet rebuker.

8. *The man will sing loudly.*
   The man will be a loud singer.

9. *Absalom rebelled against King David.*
   Absalom was an against-king-David rebel.

10. *God created heaven and earth.*
    God was the heaven and earth creator.

Exercise Seven

In the following exercise, analyze each statement. In the blank at the right, put down what sort of categorical statement it is, i.e. universal affirmative, universal negative, particular affirmative, or particular negative.

1. *Some cowboys are intellectuals.*   **Particular Affirmative**

2. *All Scripture is God-breathed writing.*   **Universal Affirmative**

3. *Some Christians are not students.*   **Particular Negative**

4. *No Christians are Hindus.*   **Universal Negative**

5. *Some books are pornography.*   **Particular Affirmative**

6. *Some writers are not Christians.*   **Particular Negative**

7. *All dogs are carnivores.*   **Universal Affirmative**

8. *No cats are musicians.*   **Universal Negative**

9. *Some soldiers are not brave men.*   **Particular Negative**

10. *All men are mortal.*   **Universal Affirmative**

With the next sentences, translate them in one of the four forms.

11. *Christians are not condemned.*
    No Christians are condemned people.

12. *Every false teacher attacks the authority of Scripture.*
    All false teachers are Scripture-authority attackers.

13. *A few churches allow divorce too easily.*
    Some churches are too easy divorce allowers.

14. *Many people do not believe in the devil.*
    Some people are not devil believers.

Exercise Eight

In the space provided, draw six squares of opposition. With the first one, at the appropriate corners, place the four categorical statements, using the abbreviations *S* and *P*. With the second square, place **A**, **E**, **I** or **O** at the appropriate corner. On the third square, enter the letters again, and draw in the appropriate lines of contradiction. On the fourth square, use *dogs* as the subject and *cats* as the predicate (so the upper left-hand corner of that square would say *All dogs are cats*).

In the last two squares, make up categorical statements of your own and place them in the appropriate corners.

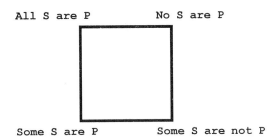

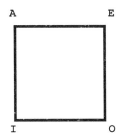

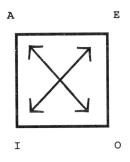

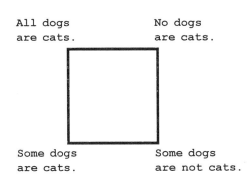

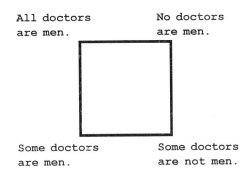

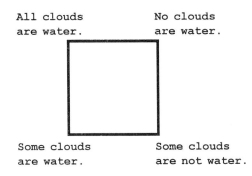

Exercise Nine

Analyze the following arguments. Each of them contain two contradictory statements. Isolate those statements (ignoring the extra), translate them into categorical statements with the same subject and predicate, and diagram where they are located on the square of opposition. Please show all your work.

1. All logic students can see the problem here. While it may be true that some of them cannot see the problem, they will if they think about it.

`All logic students`
`are problem seers.`

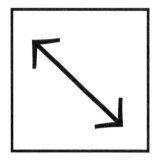

`Some logic students`
`are not problem seers.`

There is no good reason to believe that the Bible is the Word of God; it is simply the word of men. I admit that prophecies which were fulfilled is one good reason to believe it, though I am still unconvinced.

`No reasons are`
`good Bible supporters.`

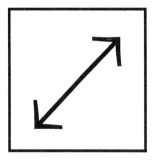

`Some reasons are`
`good Bible supporters.`

Exercise Ten

Analyze the following paragraphs, isolate the related statements, and put them into categorical form. Assign abbreviations to the terms, and place them on the square of opposition. One will show the relationship of contradiction, one the relationship of contrariety, and one subcontrariety. Show your work.

1. Johnny sneered at Billy, "All third-graders are stupid!" Billy shouted back, ineffectively countering Johnny's point, "That's not true! None of them are!"

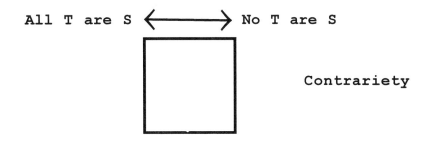

2. Smith said, "Pro-lifers don't care about children who are already born. All they care about is their stupid political agenda." Jones disagreed, "No, there are many pro-lifers who are involved in helping children."

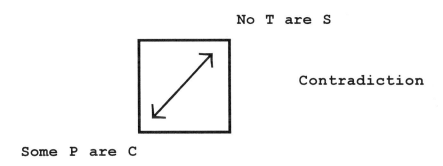

3. Some people I know are always complaining about their jobs; they never seem to quit. Of course, not everyone complains.

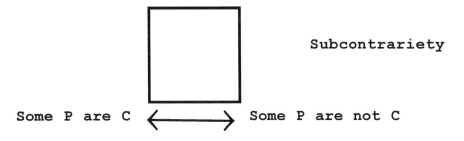

Exercise Eleven

In the following exercise, write the relationship which exists between the two given statements in the blank at right. Their order does matter.

1. *All cowboys are rough men.*
   Some cowboys are not rough men.   **Contradiction**

2. *Some ladies are not rude women.*
   No ladies are rude women.   **Superimplication**

3. *All Christians are forgiven sinners.*
   Some Christians are forgiven sinners.   **Subimplication**

4. *No Christians are Muslims.*
   Some Christians are not Muslims.   **Subimplication**

5. *All french fries are greasy food.*
   No french fries are greasy food.   **Contrariety**

6. *Some pictures are beautiful art.*
   Some pictures are not beautiful art.   **Subcontrariety**

7. *Some atheists are irrational men.*
   No atheists are irrational men.   **Contradiction**

8. *All eighth graders are brilliant logicians.*
   Some eighth graders are brilliant logicians.   **Subimplication**

9. *All violinists are right-handed players.*
   Some violinists are not right-handed players.   **Contradiction**

10. *Some feminists are feminine.*
    All feminists are feminine.   **Superimplication**

11. *All Democrats are Republicans.*
    Some Democrats are not Republicans.   **Contradiction**

12. *All conservatives are reactionaries.*
    Some conservatives are reactionaries.   **Subimplication**

Exercise Twelve

1. Draw the square of opposition, including all the arrows and relationships. Include the abbreviated categorical statements in the corners, using *S* and *P*.

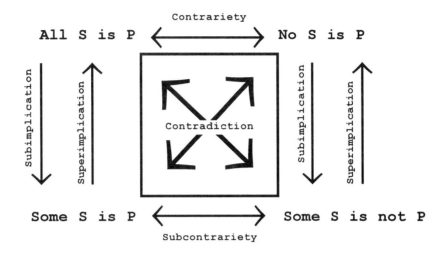

Identify the relationships between statements described.

2. One must be true and the other must be false.   **Contradiction**

3. Both can be true, but both cannot be false.   **Subcontrariety**

4. If the particular is false, its universal is false.   **Superimplication**

Write a set of statements which are related by
5. Contrariety
    All books are novels.
    No books are novels.

6. Contradiction
    All houses are buildings.
    Some houses are not buildings.

7. Subimplication
    No snakes are mammals.
    Some snakes are not mammals.

In the following problems, assume that the first statement in each set is true. Then determine the truth value of each remaining statement in the set. Circle **T** if it is true, **F** if it is false, and **?** If the truth value cannot be determined.

8. All students are young people.
   No students are young people.   T   (F)   ?
   Some students are young people.   (T)   F   ?

9. No angels are demons.
   Some angels are demons.   T   (F)   ?
   Some angels are not demons.   (T)   F   ?

10. Some computers are word processors.
    All computers are word processors.   T   F   (?)
    No computers are word processors.   T   (F)   ?

11. Some laws are not biblical laws.
    All laws are biblical laws.   T   (F)   ?
    No laws are biblical laws.   T   F   (?)

Translate the following statements into standard categorical form. Do not abbreviate.

12. Students never eat frog legs.
    No students are frog-leg eaters.

13. Many children make mud pies.
    Some children are mud-pie makers.

14. Everybody has sinned.
    All people are sinners.

15. A few of the problems were not hard.
    Some problems were not hard problems.

SYLLOGISMS AND VALIDITY

Exercise 13

Underline the conclusion in each of the following arguments.

1. All theology is a study in infinity, so <u>all calculus problems are theology</u>, because all calculus problems are a study in infinity.

2. All space stations are important research, but some space stations are not a product of American ingenuity. Therefore <u>some important research is not a product of American ingenuity</u>.

3. <u>Some pagans are idolaters</u>, because no pagans are Christians, and no Christians are idolaters.

4. All objects in free fall are weightless, and all meteorites are objects in free fall. Therefore <u>all meteorites are weightless</u>.

5. All marsupials are pouched animals, and some marsupials are not Australian mammals. Consequently, <u>some Australian mammals are not pouched animals</u>.

6. <u>Some Socratic sages are not perspicacious people</u>, since some Socratic sages are metaphorical masters, and some perspicacious people are also metaphorical masters.

7. All murderers are criminals, and some heroes of the faith were murderers, from which it follows that <u>some criminals are heroes of the faith</u>.

8. No street legal vehicles are stock cars. Thus <u>no racing car is street legal</u>, since all stock cars are racing cars.

9. <u>Some conclusions are not easily located statements</u>, for all easily located statements are sentences at the end of arguments, and some sentences at the end of arguments are not conclusions.

10. Given that some pagan literature is great writing, and no great writing is worthless instructional material, we must conclude that <u>some pagan literature is not worthless instructional material</u>.

Exercise 14

In the last section, you saw examples of valid arguments with a false premise and a true conclusion, and true premises with a true conclusion. You also saw an invalid argument with true premises and a true conclusion. In this exercise, write arguments with the given criteria.

1. Valid argument, two false premises, false conclusion:
```
All cats are dogs.
All pigs are cats.
Therefore, all pigs are dogs.
```

2. Valid argument, two false premises, true conclusion:
```
All women are at least thirty-five years old.
All U.S. presidents are women.
Thus, all U.S. presidents are at least
    thirty-five years old
```

3. Invalid argument, two false premises, false conclusion:
```
No Americans are Baptists.
No Baptists are engineers.
So all engineers are Americans.
```

4. Invalid argument, two false premises, true conclusion:
```
All bright objects are black holes.
All stars are black holes.
Therefore, some stars are bright objects.
```

5. Invalid argument, two true premises, false conclusion:
```
Some men are doctors.
Some doctors are wealthy people.
Hence, no wealthy people are men.
```

Exercise 15

Identify the major, minor and middle terms for each syllogism. The syllogisms are not necessarily in standard order.

1. All theology is a study in infinity, so all calculus problems are theology, because all calculus problems are a study in infinity.

Major: **Theology**   Minor: **Calculus problems**   Middle: **Study in infinity**

2. All space stations are important research, but some space stations are not a product of American ingenuity. Therefore some important research is not a product of American ingenuity.

Major: **Product of American ingenuity**   Minor: **Important research**   Middle: **Space relations**

3. Some pagans are idolaters, because no pagans are Christians, and no Christians are idolaters.

Major: **Idolators**   Minor: **Pagans**   Middle: **Christians**

4. All objects in free fall are weightless, and all meteorites are objects in free fall. Therefore all meteorites are weightless.

Major: **Weightless objects**   Minor: **Meteorites**   Middle: **Objects in free fall**

5. All marsupials are pouched animals, and some marsupials are not Australian mammals. Consequently, some Australian mammals are not pouched animals.

Major: **Pouched animals**   Minor: **Australian mammals**   Middle: **Marsupials**

Rewrite into standard order for categorical syllogisms:

6. Some Socratic sages are not perspicacious people, since some Socratic sages are metaphorical masters, and some perspicacious people are also metaphorical masters.

```
Some perspicacious people are metaphorical masters.
Some Socratic sages are metaphorical masters.
Therefore, some Socratic sages are not
    perpicacious people
```

7. All murderers are criminals, and some heroes of the faith were murderers, from which it follows that some criminals are heroes of the faith.

```
Some heroes of the faith were murderers.
All murderers are criminals.
Therefore, some criminals are heroes of the faith.
```

8. No street legal vehicles are stock cars. Thus no racing car is street legal, since all stock cars are racing cars.

```
No street-legal vehicles are stock cars.
All stock cars are racing cars.
Therefore, no racing car is a street legal vehicle.
```

9. Some conclusions are not easily located statements, for all easily located statements are sentences at the end of arguments, and some sentences at the end of arguments are not conclusions.

```
All easily located statements are sentences at the
    end of arguments.
Some sentences at the end of arguments are
    not conclusions.
Therefore, some conclusions are not easily
    located statements.
```

10. Given that some pagan literature is great writing, and no great writing is worthless instructional material, we must conclude that some pagan literature is not worthless instructional material.

```
No great writing is worthless instructional material.
Some pagan literature is great writing.
Therefore, some pagan literature is not worthless
    instructional material.
```

Exercise 16

Determine the form (mood and figure) of the following syllogisms and write it on the blank. The first two are in standard order, the next two are not.

1. All Bibles are books.
    Some periodicals are not books.
    Therefore some periodicals are not Bibles.   **AOO-2**

2. Some speeches are sermons.
    No sermons are short events.
    Thus some short events are not speeches.   **IEO-4**

3. Some blondes are geniuses,   `All S are G`
    because all students are geniuses,   `All B are S`
    and all blondes are students.   `Some B are G`   **AAI-1**

4. No fish are mammals,   `No F are M`
    so no snakes are mammals,   `No F are S`
    since no fish are snakes.   `No S are M`   **EEE-3**

Now develop your own syllogisms to meet the requirements of the given form. Make sure your syllogisms are in standard order.

5. **AEE-1**
```
All women are people.
No men are women.
Thus, no men are people.
```

6. **EAO-2**
```
No men are women.
All mothers are women.
Thus, some mothers are not men.
```

7. **AII-3**
```
All men are people.
Some men are lawyers.
Thus, some lawyers are people.
```

8. **OAO-4**
```
Some women are not lawyers.
All lawyers are people.
Thus, some people are not lawyers.
```

Exercise 17

Test the following syllogisms by counterexample. If no counterexample is possible, write "valid."

1. *Some cherubim are not angels.*
   Some angels are not seraphim.
   Therefore, all seraphim are cherubim.

   ```
   Some people are not angels.
   Some angels are not good beings.
   Therefore, all good beings are people.
   ```

2. *No wind instruments are guitars.*
   All wind instruments are expensive instruments.
   Therefore, no expensive instrument is a guitar.

   ```
   No watermelons are grapes.
   All watermelons are edible things.
   Therefore, no edible things are grapes.
   ```

3. *All NIV Bibles are Zondervan publications.*
   Some KJV Bibles are not Zondervan publications.
   Therefore, no KJV Bible is an NIV Bible.

   ```
   All snakes are reptiles.
   Some animals are not reptiles.
   Therefore, no animal is a snake.
   ```

4. *Some Baptists are not Presbyterians.*
   No Nazarene is a Baptist.
   Therefore, all Nazarenes are Presbyterians.

   ```
   Some bones are not plastic.
   No nectarines are bones.
   Therefore, all nectarines are plastic.
   ```

5. *All Calvinists are predestinarians.*
   No predestinarian is an Arminian.
   Therefore, some Arminians are not Calvinists.

    Valid.

6. *Some colds are not fatal diseases.*
   All cancers are fatal diseases.
   Therefore, some cancers are not colds.

    Some animals are not birds.
    All crows are birds.
    Therefore, some crows are not animals.

Challenge: Work through the 256 forms of syllogisms in the Appendix, using counterexamples to find the invalid ones. There are 232 invalid forms, and 24 valid ones. As you work through them, remember that if you cannot figure out a counterexample, it is either valid, or you need to be more creative. Also, you would be greatly assisted in working through them more quickly if you recall what you learned about relationships between statements. Good luck!

    Valid forms from appendix:

    AAA-1, AAI-1, AAI-3, AAI-4, AEE-2, AEE-4, AEO-2,
    AEO-4, AII-1, AII-3, AOO-2, EAE-1, EAE-2, EAO-1,
    EAO-2, EAO-3, EAO-4, EIO-1, EIO-2, EIO-3, EIO-4
    IAI-3, IAI-4, OAO-3

Exercise 18

In the following exercise, analyze the syllogisms. Identify which rules are violated in the syllogism by writing the name of the fallacy or fallacies. If no fallacy is made, write "valid." The premises are *not* necessarily in standard order. (Hint: the first syllogism violates three rules).

1. *Some chefs are not fat people.*
   No fat person is a contented person.
   Therefore, all chefs are contented people.   **2 Neg. Prem. &
Neg.—Aff. &
Illicit Minor**

2. *All water is blue liquid*
   No blue liquid is a solid object.
   Therefore, some water is not a solid object.   **Valid**

3. *Some Christians are not Bible-readers.*
   No Bible-reader is an ignorant person.
   Therefore, no ignorant person is a Christian.   **2 Neg. Prem.
Illicit Major**

4. *All Muslims are Hindus.*
   All Hindus are Christians.
   Therefore, some Christians are not Muslims.   **2 Aff.—Neg.**

5. *No dog is a cat.*
   Some cats are female.
   Therefore, some dogs are female.   **Neg.—Aff.**

6. *Some politicians are corrupt men.*
   Some corrupt men are Mafia members.
   Therefore, some politicians are Mafia members. **Und. Middle**

7. *No honors students are rugby players.*
   Some athletes are rugby players.
   Therefore, some athletes are not honors students.   **Valid**

8. *Some challenging games are not fun games.*
   Some fun games are not chess.
   Therefore, all challenging games are chess.   **Illicit Minor &
   Neg.—Aff. &
   2 Neg. Prem.**

9. *Some professionals are millionaires.*
   Some millionaires are not lazy men.
   Therefore, no lazy men are professionals.   **Und. Middle &
   Illicit Major**

10. *Some Baptists are immersionists.*
    No Presbyterian is a Baptist.
    Therefore some Presbyterians are not immersionists.   **Illicit Major**

ARGUMENTS IN
NORMAL ENGLISH

Exercise 19

Write two valid immediate inferences for each of the statements given. Identify the immediate inferences as either *converse*, *obverse*, or *contrapositive*.

1. All things that glitter are gold.
   No things that glitter are non-gold — Obverse
   All non-gold things are non-things that glitter — Contrapositive

2. No emperors were philosophers.
   All emperors were non-philosophers — Obverse
   No philosophers were emperors — Converse

3. Some prophets are pagans.
   Some prophets are not non-pagan — Obverse
   Some pagans are prophets — Converse

4. Some mathematicians are not teachers.
   Some mathematicians are non-teachers — Obverse
   Some non-teachers are not non-mathematicians — Contrapositive

Now translate the following arguments into standard-form categorical syllogisms. Note that they may not be in proper order. Also, find and identify the one invalid syllogism.

5. Some Christians are Calvinists, but no Christians are unbelievers. Therefore some Calvinists are believers.
   All Christians are believers.
   Some Christians are Calvinists.
   Therefore, some Calvinists are believers.

6. All mumbling is murmuring, so all mumbling is nonsensical, since no murmuring is sensical.

```
No murmuring is sense.
All mumbling is murmuring.
Therefore, no mumbling is sense.
```

7. All perfect beings are nonhuman, since all mortals are imperfect, and no humans are immortals.

```
All humans are mortals.
No mortals are perfect beings.
Therefore, no perfect beings are human.
```

8. All eighth graders are less than six-feet tall, because all poor logicians are non-eighth graders, and nobody six feet tall or more is a good logician.

```
All six-footers are poor logicians.
No poor logicians are eighth graders.
Therefore, no eight graders are six-footers.
```

9. Some non-adults are not immature people, but no mature people are impatient people. We must conclude that some adults are patient people.

```
Some mature people are not adults.
All mature people are patient people.
Therefore, some adults are patient people.
                                    INVALID
```

10. No things that glitter are non-gold, and all gold is expensive. Thus, nothing that glitters is inexpensive.

```
All gold is expensive things.
All glitterers is gold.
Therefore, all glitterers are expensive things.
```

Exercise 20

Translate the following statements in normal English into standard categorical form.

1. God is good.
   All God is good being.

2. As many as are led by the Spirit of God, these are sons of God.
   All people led by the Spirit of God are Sons of God.

3. If you sin then you are a lawbreaker.
   All sinners are lawbreakers.

4. Not everybody will come.
   Some people are not comers.

5. A soft answer turns away wrath.
   All soft answers are wrath deflectors.

6. If anyone loves the world, the love of the Father is not in him.
   No world lovers are Father lovers.

7. Many antichrists have come.
   Some antichrists have been comers.

8. I believe.
   All I am a believer.

9. The Pharisees sit in Moses' seat.
   All Pharisees are in-Moses'-seat sitters.

10. The love of most will grow cold.
    Some love will be cold love.

Exercise 21

Translate the following statements in normal English into standard categorical form.

1. Wherever you go, there you are.
    All places you go are places where you are.

2. You may prepare it however you like.
    All ways you like are ways you may prepare it.

3. Unless you repent, you too will perish.
    All unrepentant people will be perishers.

4. He never did anything wrong.
    No times are times he did wrong.

5. You will reap what you sow.
    All things you sow are things you will reap.

6. He gets sick whenever he drinks milk.
    All times he drinks milk are times he gets sick.

7. Righteousness is found only in the Lord.
    All righteousness is a thing found in the Lord.

8. God does whatever He pleases.
    All things God pleases are things God does.

9. You always hurt the one you love.
    All people you love are people you hurt.

10. Nobody leaves except those who have finished.
    No non-finishers are leavers; All finishers are leavers.

Translate the following arguments into standard categorical form.

11. Happy is the land that has no history, and King Frank's land has no history. We must conclude that King Frank's land is happy.

```
All history-free lands are happy lands.
All King Frank's land is history-free land.
Therefore, all King Frank's land is a happy land.
```

12. None but the wise are truly happy, so Solomon was happy, since he was so wise.

```
All happy people are wise people.
All Solomon was a wise person.
Therefore, all Solomon was happy.
```

13. Some people are not Christ's disciples, for whoever turns away cannot be His disciple, and many people turn away.

```
No turners away are Christ's disciples.
Some people are turners away.
Therefore, some people are not Christ's disciples.
```

14. All sciences except logic study the tangible, and chemistry is not logic. Thus, chemistry is a study of the tangible.

```
All non-logic sciences are tangible studies.
All chemistry is a non-logic science.
Therefore, all chemistry is a tangible study.
```

15. *Write a counterexample to the one invalid argument on this page.*

```
Number 12 is invalid. Here is a counterexample:

All women are people.
All Solomon was a person.
Therefore, all Solomon was a woman.
```

Exercise 22

Translate the following enthymemes into standard-form syllogisms. Assume the enthymeme is valid, and place parentheses around the assumed statement.

1. Tomorrow is not Tuesday, therefore tomorrow we will not have a test.
   ```
   (All test days are Tuesday.)
   No tomorrow is Tuesday.
   Therefore, no tomorrow is a test day.
   ```

2. No enthymemes are complete, so some arguments are incomplete.
   ```
   No enthymemes are complete syllogisms.
   (Some arguments are enthymemes.)
   Therefore, some arguments are not complete syllogisms.
   ```

3. Some young people are not rebels, since not everyone rebels as a teenager.
   ```
   Some teenagers are not rebels.
   (All teenagers are young people.)
   Therefore, some young people are not rebels.
   ```

4. Most Russians are not capitalists, because communists are not capitalists.
   ```
   No communists are capitalists.
   (Some Russians are communists.)
   Therefore, some Russians are not capitalists.
   ```

5. God does whatever He pleases, and He is pleased to save sinners. So...
   ```
   All things God pleases are things God does.
   Some things God pleases is the salvation of sinners.
   (Therefore, some salvation of sinners is a thing
       God does.)
   ```

Do the same for these enthymemes, all taken from scripture.

6. "This man is not from God, for he does not keep the Sabbath" (John 9:16).
```
(All men from God are Sabbath keepers.)
No this man is a Sabbath keeper.
Therefore, no this man is a man from God.
```

7. "I will fear no evil, for you are with me" (Psalm 23:4).
```
(No people with God are evil fearers.)
All I am a person with God.
Therefore, no I am an evil fearer.
```

8. "You are worthy, our Lord and God, to receive glory . . . for you created all things" (Rev. 4:11).
```
(All creators of all things are beings worthy of glory.)
All God is a creator of all things.
Therefore, all God is a being worthy of glory.
```

9. "The promise comes by faith, so that it may be by grace" (Rom. 4:16).
```
(All things by faith are things by grace.)
All the promise is a thing by faith.
Therefore, all the promise is a thing by grace.
```

10. "Here are my mother and my brothers! For whoever does the will of my Father in heaven is my brother and sister and mother" (Matt. 12:49-50).
```
All people who do the Father's will are
     my family members.
(Some people here are people who do the
  . Father's will.)
Therefore, some people here are my family members.
```

Challenge: John 8:47 is a complete syllogism. Translate it into categorical form, and determine its validity.
```
All people of God are hearers of God.
No you are people of God.
Therefore, no you are hearers of God.

As it stands it appears invalid, which means our syl-
logism must be missing something. If we add Christ's
assumption, "All hearers of God are people of God,"
then we see that it is valid.
```

Exercise 23

Analyze each of the following arguments. In the appropriate blank, write down what form of argument it is: pure hypothetical, modus ponens, modus tollens, asserting the consequent, or denying the antecedent.

1. *If you are lazy, then you will be poor. Henry is poor, and it follows that he is therefore lazy.*   `Asserting the consequent`

2. *The Bible teaches that if a man is generous, then he will prosper. We know that Mike is not generous, and therefore cannot prosper.*   `Denying the antecedent`

3. *If you speak too much, sin will not be absent. If sin is not absent, then it is present. Thus if you speak to much, sin is present.*   `Pure hypothetical`

4. *If a ministry is of God, then it will succeed. The Mormon church is successful, and we can conclude that it is blessed by God.*   `Asserting the consequent`

5. *If you are kind to the poor, then you are lending to the Lord. Paul is kind to the poor. He is therefore lending to the Lord.*   `Modus ponens`

6. *If you visit your neighbor too much he will get sick of you. My neighbor is not sick of me, so I don't think I visit too much.*   `Modus tollens`

7. *If you don't answer a fool according to his folly, then he will think that he is wise. Sharon did not answer him that way. He must think he is wise.*   `modus ponens`

8. *If a country is rebellious, it has many rulers. Argentina has had many rulers; it must be a rebellious country.*   `Asserting the consequent`

9. *If a man is lawless, even his prayers are detestable. Larry is not at all a lawless man. So his prayers must not be detestable.*   `Denying the antecedent`

10. *"If you are willing, you can make me clean."*
"I am willing," Jesus said. "Be clean."   `Modus ponens`

11. *If recycling were necessary, then it would*
be profitable. Recycling is not yet profitable.
So it must not be necessary.   `Modus tollens`

12. *If a man gives gifts, then everyone wants to*
be his friend. Everyone wants to be Gordon's
friend. Gordon must give out a lot of gifts.   `Asserting the consequent`

13. *If they receive you they receive me. If they receive*
me, then they receive Him who sent me. So if they
receive you, they receive Him who sent me.   `Pure hypothetical`

14. *If I killed you, then you would be dead. I*
promise that I will never kill you. Therefore,
you will never die!   `Denying the antecedent`

15. *If you flog a mocker, then the simple will learn*
prudence. We don't flog mockers. That must
be why we have so many imprudent people.   `Denying the antecedent`

16. *If you are rich, then many will want to be*
your friend. No one wants to be Jessica's friend.
She must not be rich.   `Modus tollens`

17. *If you honor the Lord with your wealth, then*
He will bless you greatly. Mr. Spence has always
honored the Lord this way. He will be blessed.   `Modus ponens`

18. *If you fear the Lord, then you will love*
wisdom. A man who hates wisdom must not
fear the Lord.   `Modus tollens`

19. *If you are a Christian, then you will read*
your Bible. I know a man who reads the Bible.
He must be a Christian.   `Asserting the consequent`

20. *If they had belonged to us, they would*
have remained with us. But they went out from
us. This showed that they did not belong to us.   `Modus tollens`

Exercise 24

Analyze the following paragraph. Separate the various arguments (there are four), and determine whether they are valid or not. Identify each argument by name.

If Paul went to Ephesus, then he wouldn't write the Ephesians a letter. But he did write them a letter, which means that he didn't go to Ephesus. But if Paul didn't go to Ephesus, then he would not have known the people there. We know, however that Paul did go to Ephesus, therefore he did know the people there. If he knew the people in Ephesus, then he would have known the saints in Colossae too. But we know that he did not know the Christians in Colossae, which means that he didn't know the Ephesians. If Paul didn't know the Ephesians, then he would have written them a letter. He wrote them a letter, and this proves that he did not know them.

1. E ⊃ L
   ~L ∴ ~E

   Modus tollens, valid

2. E ⊃ K
   ~E ∴ ~K

   Denying the antecedent, invalid

3. E ⊃ C
   ~C ∴ ~E

   Modus tollens, valid

4. K ⊃ W
   W ∴ K

   Asserting the consequent, invalid

INFORMAL FALLACIES

Exercise 25

Identify the fallacy of distraction which is being made in each of the following examples.

1. *Oswald must have been the lone assassin of* Kennedy. Nobody has ever been able to prove *any of the conspiracy theories.*　　　**ad ignoratium**

2. *Vote YES! for our schools. Don't deny children* *a decent education.*　　　**ad populum**

3. *Santa Claus must be real. The editor of the* newspaper said so.　　　**ipse dixit**

4. *You believe in Jesus because you were* *brought up in a Christian home.*　　　**Bulverism**

5. *We need to appropriate billions of dollars for AIDS* research. Otherwise, you or someone in your family *will probably get AIDS within the next ten years.*　　　**ad baculum**

6. *You don't believe that Genesis is to be under-* stood literally, do you? That's a rather old- *fashioned doctrine.*　　　**chronological snobbery**

7. *We should say the pledge of allegiance at our* *assemblies just like every other school does.*　　　**ad populum**

8. *A heretic named Servetus was burned at the* stake in Geneva, and John Calvin approved of it. Calvinism has to be wrong.　　　**ad hominem**

9. *You can't tell me it's wrong to cheat. You've* *cheated before too!*　　　**tu quoque**

10. *Do you disagree with me when I say that* mankind is corrupt? That proves that you have *been corrupted already.*　　　**ad hominem**

11. *The senator is accused of communist activities, and there is nothing to disprove these suspicions.*   **ad ignoratium**

12. *You should read this book that your boss wrote. You would not want to jeopardize your position in this company, would you?*   **ad baculum**

13. *The vice-president said that potato is spelled with an "e" at the end, so it must be true.*   **ipse dixit**

14. *Professor Pepper thinks teachers should get paid more so they won't leave teaching for other jobs. But he's a teacher himself, so that figures.*   **Bulverism**

15. *My dad tells me that I shouldn't shoplift, but I don't listen to him, because I happen to know that he stole candy from stores when he was a kid.*   **tu quoque**

16. *Of course God exists. Belief in a deity is one of the most ancient concepts of man.*   **chronological snobbery**

Exercise 26

Name the fallacies of ambiguity being made in the following examples.

1. Mother, you told me not to take any cookies.
I didn't *take* them anywhere, I ate them right here.   **accent**

2. *Super Frosted Sugar Bombs* must be nutritious,
because they are part of this nutritious breakfast.   **division**

3. My friend said that he hit his head on a rock,
breaking it into a million pieces. But I don't think
anyone could live with a shattered head!   **amphiboly**

4. Teacher: "I instructed you to write a letter to
someone, and you haven't done it." Student:
"Yes I did. I wrote the letter *A*."   **equivocation**

5. Jesus taught that we should love our *neighbor*.
So it's okay to hate the people across town.   **accent**

6. If two teaspoons of sugar make this taste good,
then four will make it taste twice as good!   **composition**

7. Bread and water is better than nothing, but
nothing is better than a steak dinner. So bread
and water is better than a steak dinner.   **equivocation**

8. American Indians are disappearing. But that
man is an American Indian, so he must be
disappearing, too!   **division**

9. I read on the front page, "Grandmother of
Eight Makes Hole in One." Her poor grandchild!   **amphiboly**

10. "Mary had a little lamb." I'll bet the doctor was
surprised.   **equivocation**

Exercise 27

Identify the following fallacies of form by name.

1. *You can tear the front page of the phone book in half, so you should be able to tear the whole phone book in half.*

apriorism

2. *President Schwartz was just elected, and the stock market soared to new heights. I'm glad I voted for him.*

post hoc ergo propter hoc

3. *"Have you stopped getting drunk all the time?" "No!" "Oh, so you admit to being a drinker!"*

complex question

4. *Rotten Banana is a great band. I know, because all the cool kids like them. Which are the cool kids? The ones who like Rotten Banana, of course!*

petitio principii

5. *That guy from the community church reads all the time. They must all be bookworms out there.*

apriorism

6. *If you leave the Christian school, then you will have to go to the public schools.*

either/or

7. *I didn't study because I had to go to church. I got an A on the test anyway. I'm going to go to church before tests more often.*

post hoc ergo propter hoc

8. *Miracles don't happen because that would violate natural law, and natural law cannot be violated.*

petitio principii

9. *She killed the wicked witch of the east. So she must either be a good witch, or a bad witch.*

either/or

10. *Ever since I started eating seaweed with my meals, I haven't gotten sick once. You should eat it, too!*

post hoc ergo propter hoc

Exercise 28

Identify the fallacies made in the examples below. They can be any of the fallacies of distraction, ambiguity, or form.

1. The chain letter read, "If you don't keep this letter going, you may lose your job, get in an accident, or go bald!"   `ad baculum`

2. That chain letter was real. Just a week after I threw it away, I failed my logic test.   `post hoc ergo propter hoc`

3. My girlfriend always keep chain letters going. She says that nobody has proven to her that they don't really work.   `ad ignoratium`

4. A recycling poster said, "Recycle cans and waste paper," so I am wasting paper every chance I get!   `amphiboly`

5. All my friends recycle their cans, so it must be a good thing to do.   `ad populum`

6. I read that "Life is either a daring adventure, or nothing." My life certainly isn't a daring adventure, so I guess it's nothing.   `either/or`

7. The apostle Paul told us to honor our leaders. But he dishonored the high priest, so why should I listen to him?   `tu quoque`

8. Honoring your leaders is an old tradition that no longer applies to our modern, sophisticated age.   `chronological snobbery`

9. The Japanese always score higher on math than the Americans. So I am sure our Japanese neighbor can help you with your calculus.   `division`

10. The Japanese are better at math because
they're smarter. We know that they're smarter,
because they always do better at math.   **petitio principii**

11. Hi, I am selling tickets to the policeman's ball,
and I am sure you would like to support your local
police, so will it be cash, check or credit card?   **complex question**

12. Of course the Joint-Chiefs-of-Staff say we ought
to increase military spending. As members of the
armed forces, they want as much as they can get.   **Bulverism**

13. We shouldn't listen to Senator Slug either,
since we all know he is a card-carrying member
of the radical right.   **ad hominem**

14. Oh, so you believe in evolution? Tell me, are
you descended from a monkey on your mother's
side or your father's side?   **either/or; ad hom.**

15. The world was not created by God, for matter
has always existed, and thus needs no God to
explain where it came from.   **petitio principii**

16. The press has a duty to publish what is clearly
in the public interest. And there is certainly public
interest in the private life of the rich and famous.   **equivocation**

17. I had a bad time with my former husband.
Trust me deary, men are no good.   **apriorism**

18. The idea of trying to colonize Mars is ridiculous.
My mother, my boss, and my wife all agreed it
couldn't possibly work.   **ipse dixit**

19. Each snowflake is so light. There is no way
that snow could make that roof collapse.   **composition**

20. That last guy said snowflakes were light. But
I always thought that snow was made of water.   **equivocation**

Notes